DAUGHTER

&

SON

Cassandra Medley

BROADWAY PLAY PUBLISHING INC
New York
www.broadwayplaypublishing.com
info@broadwayplaypublishing.com

DAUGHTER and SON
© Copyright 2011 by Cassandra Medley

First printing: July 2011
I S B N: 978-0-88145-478-9

Book design: Marie Donovan
Page make-up: Adobe Indesign
Typeface: Palatino
Printed and bound in the U S A

CONTENTS

DAUGHTER

DAUGHTER was originally produced in the Ensemble Studio Maraton in June 2009. The cast and creative contributor were:

MONIQUE..Kaliswa Brewster
LOUISE .... Lynn Matthew
VIOLA..Natalie Carter
ALMA ....Gayle Samuels

Director .... Petronia Paley

CHARACTERS & SETTING

MONIQUE, *African-American woman, aged 19. Pretty, vivacious, boldly venturing into life.*

ALMA, MONIQUE's *mother. African-American, late 40s, early 50s.*

LOUISE, ALMA's *neighbor and close friend. African-American, late 40s, early 50s.*

VIOLA, ALMA's *neighbor and close friend. African-American, late 40s, early 50s.*

Play takes place in ALMA's *mind and memory: her church sanctuary and basement, her daughter's bedroom, a construction site, her car.*

Scene

(Gospel choir is heard—morning of the funeral.)

(LOUISE and VIOLA emerge from the shadows in choir robes, singing a Gospel melody as part of a church choir. Grief-stricken)

(ALMA stands up suddenly, surprising the choir, who come to a pause.)

ALMA: Want y'all to know how grateful I am are for all your cards and calls and prayers. Amen! Want you to know that I'm still carrying on in faith...the Lord's will be done. As Reverend has just told us, God's ways are—passed our understanding....

CHURCH CONGREGANTS: Amen.

(ALMA in spotlight. LOUISE and VIOLA fade into the shadows.)

(Lights convey feeling of flashback. We hear MONIQUE's voice off-stage.)

MONIQUE: *(Offstage)* Mommie?

Scene

(MONIQUE enters, pretty,vivacious.)

MONIQUE: Mom, whatsamatter?

(ALMA is taken aback. She immediately caresses MONIQUE's face. MONIQUE steps back, bewildered.)

(ALAM bursts in to exuberant laughter.)

ALMA: *(Raising hands on high)*Thank you, Jesus!! Thank you!!! *(To* MONIQUE*)* I been having this horrible nightmare, see? You was... you was...

MONIQUE: *(Smiling, quizzical, warm)* Mom, you can be so wack at times.

ALMA: Girl, get in the car.

MONIQUE: Where we going?

ALMA: We getting you up to Canada!

MONIQUE: Canada. Oh...we're no the new Underground Railroad that you dreamed about. I remember granddaddy's slavery stories 'bout our family escaping to Canda on the Underground Railroad.

ALMA: You know that's the truth. It's like there's a new Underground Railroad, see? This one girl, white girl, up in—where was she from—she went A-WOL up to Canada...and this other young man, white, him too... and...and...a couple others...

MONIQUE: Momma, what you planning in your head?

ALMA: *(To* MONIQUE *as she drives)* You've had a change of mind! This what I should've pushed you to do from the start!! I should've paid for your college, somehow, some way.. And now, we gonna really and truly do it, see? Relax... just take it nice 'n easy...

MONIQUE: Now you know good and well how you hate doing anything illegal.

ALMA: Pretend we're just going over to Windsor to Mount Olivet Presbyterian to sing a recital. Here we go...crossing the bridge, now...Detroit River...look down...so sparkling...promise you'll get word to me how you doing. Remember NEVER use your credit card just in case they try and trace you...we on our way to Canada, like I really, deep down wanted to take you!!...

MONIQUE: That won't make it real.

ALMA: Maybe you'll find a way to go to school up there.

MONIQUE: We're breaking the law.

ALMA: Hell with the law, dammit.

MONIQUE: Thing is. I signed up. I signed on the "dotted line."

ALMA: Gotta get you cross that Bridge!! I WILL get you across—to hell with what anybody thinks about it!!

MONIQUE: Anything can happen. It's your dream.

ALMA: QUIT IT. TALK SENSE! *(Pointing)* Checkpoint coming up—we going to cross this bridge over to the—do you understand me! Now...they not gonna mess with good Christian folks, see— We'll get you to Toronto—get you to one of them sanctuary churches— in Toronto. Get ready, get my license out m'purse for I D...!

(Suddenly a zooming, thunderous boom)

(ALMA attempts to clutch onto MONIQUE, then ALMA moves off from the scene.)

(ALMA stands in a spotlight.)

ALMA: No! NO!! NO!! NO! NO!!!

(Lights go to black and swirling spotlights, voices heard over exploding bombs gunfire, more explosions ALMA stands in spotlight.)

(Lights shift.)

Scene

(Spotlight, MONIQUE *seated in spotlight, head covered in bandages, moaning and panting.)*

MONIQUE: *(Having a nightmare)* It's a *baby*!! Back up... no! Stop! The bump is a baby!!!

*(*ALMA *rushes over to* MONIQUE, *grabs her by the shoulders, rocking her.)*

ALMA: Sh-h-h-h-h... Wake up, darling... You're back in the States, beloved. Momma's right here.

MONIQUE: *(Waking up)* What happened to my face?

ALMA: You home, now, you're here! Safe and sound and back home,you're right here!!

*(*MONIQUE *wakes up, clings to* ALMA.*)*

MONIQUE: Where's "here"???

ALMA: "Here"is with Momma. Here is with me.

Scene

*(*ALMA*'s church. the sanctuary—a Sunday afternoon)*

(Sound of a large church choir finishing a rousing gospel song)

(Enter LOUISE *and* VIOLA *dressed in choir robes.* ALMA *joins them.* VIOLA *ends the song, then:)*

VIOLA: AMEN!!

(Sounds of applause, and clapping)

LOUISE: "The Monique Richardson Fund Drive," Folks!

*(*ALMA *is surprised and deeply gratified.)*

VIOLA: Look at her shock, everybody!! We been planning!

(Sounds of crowd laughter, clapping and crowd applause)

(LOUISE *takes up a hand-held mike.*)

LOUISE: Now then, we've all read in the news about our choir member, here Sister Alma Richardson, and her daughter Monique's sacrifice to her country and we're proud!!

VIOLA: Halleluyah. One thing about Southwest Detroit—we're a community, a caring community!! Right on, and A-men! You KNOW that's right! Let us all say, Amen!

CROWD: *(Sound)* AMEN!!

(*Clapping, loud applause.* ALMA *takes the mike.*)

ALMA: A-men. My goodness. Excuse me, I'm a little blown away...still jet lagged. Everything's been happening so. Quick. Can't keep up. One second, I get a phone call...then 'fore I know nothing, I'm at that Walter Reed Hospital, walking down that long, long hallway, holding my cross in my hand, opening the door to see...my beloved girl... (*Falls into a daze*)

(LOUISE *and* VIOLA *exchange glances,* VIOLA *takes the mike.*)

VIOLA: We got folks from Visger Road to Outer Drive—and not just our church—even the Catholic church and the Jehovah Witnesses, and Fort Street Presbyterian, Church of God in Christ. And Temple Sinai has sent in funds from the Jewish Community!

ALMA: (*Takes the mike*) Everybody...now, I'm not gonna bore you with all the rigmarole, of all the bureaucratic red tape that me and Monique been having to go through...what happened to all the reassurances from the V A? Don't get me started.

(VIOLA *grabs the mike from* ALMA.)

VIOLA: Let's just say that if I *did* curse...Jesus, forgive me for even saying so in his holy house, praise God, but if I *did*—whoo, i could tell you some choice words. Not wanting to pay for the reconstruction of Moni's face!!!

(LOUISE *signals* VIOLA *to "pipe down"*, VIOLA *hands the mike back to* ALMA.)

ALMA: *(Clapping)* But we MOVING FORWARD cause we got Je-sus on our side, church!! We NEVER gonna give up hoping and praying, A-men.

VIOLA: We gonna collect the funds we need and keep on keeping on! *(Clapping)* A-men!! And we having us a bake sale and a garage sale, and bargain basement sale.... Ain't this wonderful!!

ALMA: This is Wonderful people! Wonderful! Just Wonderful!! We gonna have all of Moni's rehab and reconstructive surgery paid for. Thank you, Reverend Thomas and Everybody! Thank you! Thank you, Church. And my wonderful choir members, God Bless everyone!

VIOLA: We asking you to—to- open each and every heart, Lord on this day, and I'm gonna say it, with Reverend Thomas' permission, open each and every pocket, purse, wallet, checkbook, Jesus *(Revving up)* That's right!

(MONIQUE *steps into the spotlight—a "vision" in* ALMA's *mind—*MONIQUE *is groping to find her way.)*

VIOLA: I'm calling on your holy name, Lord! We asking contributions this afternoon! We know that thy will be done!
We know that...though we may be humble, simple people, Lord, every dime, every quarter, every penny...

(VIOLA *is silently signaled to by* LOUISE *to "wrap it up".)*

VIOLA: ...counts and will be blessed... *(Rushing)* ...do all this in Jesus name, Amen!

CROWD: *(Sound)* AMEN!

ALMA: *(To church)* Church, I'm strong in my faith, Church. How me and my daughter gonna live together in that house, if not with Jesus?

MONIQUE: Momma, when you dream about me, do I still have my old face?

(ALMA grabs onto LOUISE.)

ALMA: *(To church)* Let it never be said that Sister Alma lost her faith and was defeated!

LOUISE: 'Course you not gonna be "defeated"!

VIOLA: You believe in Jesus, how can you be defeated? *(She immediately begins this rousing version of gospel song.)*

(VIOLA and LOUISE fade into the background as ALMA steps forward and fervently embraces MONIQUE.)

(Lights cross fade.)

Scene

(MONIQUE sips from a cup of juice with a straw.)

ALMA: Let's open up the blinds so you can feel the sunshine. *(She mimes raising blinds.)* There. How's that feel?

MONIQUE: *(Chuckling)* How's that feel on my face?*(Pause. She gropes the air.)* Mom...

ALMA: I'm here "lollipop", Momma's right here. Moni? Y'know...when your ready we can talk about... anything you wanna talk about. Any time you want. What happened with that..."thing" that happened over there? *(Silence)* I still believe...once you get the basic healing over with—

MONIQUE: *(Interupting)* Some more stitching. more patching. More quilting...more traces and tracks across what used to be my face?

ALMA: Baby, you...ya can't stay cooped up in this here bedroom..

MONIQUE: Who says I can't?

ALMA: Terrance called.

MONIQUE: Thought you promised not to bring up his name.

ALMA: Well, I, I dunno, I...I...

MONIQUE: You promised!

ALMA: There was no need to send his ring back. *(Silence)* How 'bout we listen to the radio? *(Silence)* You could sit out on the porch, get some real sun. Get outta this bedroom and—and— *(Silence)* Remember what they tole us.

MONIQUE: Why you pushing and pushing—stop pestering me. *(Rushes off, comes back with pamphlets)*

ALMA: What about these here Braille books, how 'bout we start off with—

MONIQUE: Momma... You dream last night?

ALMA: Mmmmm.

MONIQUE: 'Bout me? *(Silence)* Did I have my old face?

(Cross fade)

Scene

(Construction site—afternoon)

*(*ALMA *in spotlight)*

(Loud sounds of building construction fade up, then are muted)

ALMA: Hi Terry! *(Pause)* Boy, aren't you looking all handsome and carrying on, just lookit you! ha! Like the mustache, it really makes you look more mature, really flatters your face, you "handsome devil, you", ha. *(Face changes. Pause)* Oh, I'm good, I'm good. Good to see ya. Look, I don't mean to come out here to bother you on your job on your lunch hour or nothing...Listen... you and me could always "talk" —you know how much I depended on you to come by all them months when Moni was in service...you and me always been good good buddies right? like you've always heard me say, I've always considered all y'all kids dropping by the house all down through the years, as one of "Momma Alma's children". And then with you and Moni ending up getting together I was so proud! *(Pause)* Eh? Oh, you gotta get back, okay! okay. Yeah, just came by to... to let you know Moni's doing well, recuperating day by day...recuperating...Terry, please. Please. I know—I know—I know... Monique, she's the one sent ya ring back...I know that. But don't give up so easy!! Please Terry... look at the way you two both said you *love* each other so—you was so looking forward to her getting back from Bagdad—soon as Moni heals there can be HOPE!! I believe that!! I believe that sure as I believe in God! Soon as she heals...I believe you won't mind a woman with a—a—a— "different looking" — "appearance" ...I mean, she's the love of your life!!! Ain't that what you've always told me!! Well!!!!??? The "love of your life", right! Right!!!!!! *(Suddenly)* Oh. Right. Right. Don't wanna cause you no trouble on your job. I'm sorry...just that I can't seem to find you nowhere else but here...sorry... promise me you'll keep calling...? Oh—oh... Right...you take care...take good care... see you later... *(Feebly playful)* ...long as one day I "will" be seeing you...Terrance...wasn't she so pretty in her African print dress?

Scene

(Lights shift, the party, Summer 2003)

(ALMA's bedroom, MONIQUE and ALMA stand before an imaginary mirror, MONIQUE wears a lovely dress, pretty as she was in past.)

ALMA: Lookit you!!! looking good go on with ya baddself!..

MONIQUE: You lookin kinda cute, too, for a ole lady.

(ALMA playfully bumps butts with MONIQUE, then hands her a small box.)

ALMA: These'll go with it. Happy Birthday.

(MONIQUE pulls out a pair of earrings and puts them on.)

MONIQUE: Ahhh! *(She kisses ALMA on the cheek.)* Thank you, Mommie.

(ALMA quickly refers to MONIQUE in the mirror.)

ALMA: Girl, you sure nough got that shapely shape. And I'm sure I know who's quite satisfied about it!

(MONIQUE gives a charming silent smile, they hold a "knowing look".)

ALMA: Don't you dare walk down that aisle before you get your college degree. Promise you won't throw away your opportunities. Promise me!

MONIQUE: Mot-her, first of all, I am not you, okay? And second, he hasn't even asked me.

ALMA: I assume you're using birth control—plus keeping him in a "rain coat," you know what I mean.

MONIQUE: *(Astonished)* Mot-her!

ALMA: "Mot-her!"

MONIQUE: Thought you don't believe in you-know-what before marriage? As a Christian?

ALMA: Are you? Never mind what I believe.

(VIOLA's voice calls from offstage.)

VIOLA: WHOO-HOO, WHERE'S EVERYBODY!?

ALMA: IN HERE GETTING DRESSED!

(VIOLA enters, still speaking to someone offstage.)

VIOLA: Leroy, take the food on into the kitchen before you turn on the T V! *(She turns to ALMA.)* I tell you, when it comes to the N F L that man's worse than a junkie! *(To MONIQUE)* Sweet dress *(Kisses her)* Happy birthday. *(She hands her a small box.)* It's a silver cross for you to have on you. Reverend Thomas blessed it.

MONIQUE: Thanks, Miz Vi. But y'all don't gotta be so solemn. It's gonna be fine. *(She sees others offstage, runs off.)* Stephanie and Bo-Bo, come on in! Hey, Terry, hey baby!!

(Sounds of people in other room, and music—2003-era R & B)

VIOLA: *(To ALMA)* Gir-r-rl, be glad you stayed single, 'cause marriage don't turn out to be nothing but, fix my plate, turn on T V, and we can't afford it.

ALMA: What about the "slam-bam-thank you m'am" part?

VIOLA: Chile, the only thing getting "serviced" at my house is the washing machine...

(LOUISE enters with camera.)

LOUISE: "Cheese" everybody, say "CHEESE". (*She snaps a quick photo herself,* VIOLA *and* ALMA.) This way she'll have all three of us at her bedside when she over there.)

(MONIQUE *enters excited, holds up an i-Pod Nano.*)

MONIQUE: Momma, lookit what Stephanie, and Ayesha, and Gail chipped in a got for me!!!

(LOUISE *hands* MONIQUE *a small box.*)

LOUISE: Happy birthday, baby.

(LOUISE *kisses* MONIQUE.)

MONIQUE: Aaagh! Thanks, God-mommie.

LOUISE: It's a mini Bible for you to carry

VIOLA: (*To* MONIQUE) That'll be good for when you go off tomorrow to Basic.

LOUISE: Never mind tomorrow, let's focus on her birthday *today*, Vi.

VIOLA: ...And then on into battle.

ALMA: Ain't nobody going into no "battle." (*To* VIOLA) Where'd you get that from.

LOUISE: (*To* VIOLA) See, now you done got Alma all upset and carrying on.

MONIQUE: Mom, it's just a figure of speech

ALMA: "Figure" of nothing! Recruiter promised, assured us!!

(MONIQUE *grabs* ALMA *by shoulders.*)

MONIQUE: Hey! What you getting yaself all in a twist about, huh?

LOUISE: Exactly. Everybody know *we* don't do like the terrorists. We don't put our women into combat.

MONIQUE: Exactly!

(Consoling and firm to ALMA*)*

VIOLA: She gonna do her time, and they'll take care of her scholarship "dime."

ALMA: A-Men!

(They all slap hands.)

MONIQUE: Be back home in no time, and then on to my pediatric nursing training, y'all. College debt-free, thanks to "Uncle Sammy". *(To* ALMA*)* Momma let's serve the food. *(To others)* What y'all wanna drink? *(She goes off.)*

LOUISE: *(To* ALMA*)* Not scared of nothing is she?

ALMA: You know Moni.

LOUISE: Tell you one thing—every time I look into the faces of the Arab kids in my classroom—and then think about my God-baby being over there—

VIOLA: I'm telling you! Why we gotta sacrifice all the time so that other folks can have democracy? I mean, we *still* go try and help these here A-rabs after all this 9-11 mess they done put us through!

ALMA: All I know is my child is gonna leaving after tonight, that's all I care about.

LOUISE: God's gonna be with her every step.

(Sounds of screaming and laughter, and clapping. The women glance offstage. MONIQUE *enters holds out her hand to show off engagement ring to* ALMA, LOUISE *and* VIOLA.*)*

MONIQUE: *(Playfully re the ring)* Uh, excuse me... excuse me!!!

ALMA: My-my-my!!

VIOLA: So, Terrance is in luvvvv!

ALMA: With a rock that size, he's at least in a trance!

MONIQUE: Mother!!

ALMA: "Muther"!

(They all laugh.)

ALMA: Know one thing—they gonna wait till she gets back from "over there" and AFTER they both get at least through college undergrad before—

MONIQUE: *(Interupthing)* Yes-yes-yes

ALMA: *(Interupting)* —and Terry's parents will agree.

(Doorbell sound)

MONIQUE: YALL COME ON IN, EVERYBODY! *(She exits.)*

VIOLA: Alma. Looka here. You stick to your guns 'bout the schooling after the military.

ALMA: They promise—she'll be kept in the Green Zone working in "telecommunications".

VIOLA: See? And this way, you're guaranteed that she won't be bringing you no Grand-babies till *after* she and Terry get to the altar.

LOUISE: Viola!

VIOLA: What? Well, look what happened to my Stephanie.

LOUISE: Tonight's my god-child's last night 'fore shipping off to Basic, and here you running your mouth.

VIOLA: *(To ALMA)* Anyway, Condi, and Mister Powell say it's gonna all blow over in six months. *(She suddenly calls offstage.)* STEPHANIE! *(To ALMA)* Lord, ha' mercy, my child! All big-bellied and not a man in sight!

LOUISE: C'mon, ya'll let's go eat.

VIOLA: And lookit pretty Monique, beauty with a head on her shoulders, handsome fiancée...

ALMA: She's a lovely girl, Stephie. Lovely eyes.

VIOLA: Why is it that when a girl is plain, they say always say she's "got lovely eyes".

(LOUISE *gently pushes* VIOLA *out.*)

LOUISE: C'mon, let's fix ya plate.

(LOUISE *and* VIOLA *exit. Lights change, party sounds instantly stop.* ALMA *turns away steps into spotlight.*)

ALMA: My baby's eyes. No more eyes. Okay, Jesus. All my life I been taught to call on your Holy Name. All my life I done what I was taught...so, I'm calling on you now...

Scene

(ALMA *moves into a spotlight. It is months later.*)

(LOUISE *enters, anxious.*)

LOUISE: Alma?

(ALMA *rushes over to* LOUISE.)

ALMA: Girl-girl-girl-girl-girl!!!!! Sorry to bother you.

LOUISE: Chile, quit! All you gotta do is call me, any time, any day. Now, what's this email all about?

(ALMA *pulls out sheets of printed paper.* LOUISE *reads.*)

ALMA: They *promised* she'd be kept in the Green Zone, working in telecommunications!! They promised!!

(LOUISE *continues to read,* ALMA *waits.*)

LOUISE: (*Shaking her head re what she reads*) Umph.

ALMA: (*Indicating on paper*) You *believe* it!!!??

LOUISE: Moni's driving Humvees...? *Monique?*

(ALMA *presents a second paper.*)

ALMA: That ain't all, honey, that ain't all.

(LOUISE *takes the second paper and reads.*)

LOUISE: *(Reading out loud)* ..."Ordered to shoot down everything and anything...even dogs."

ALMA: They promised. She suppose to be "typing", not "shooting".

LOUISE: Let's keep calm. Let's keep calm...

ALMA: I can't see my child lying to me...but still and all...the news on T V don't say our side be gunning down all these whole families, like she's talking 'bout!

LOUISE: She's fighting them "insurgents". It's hard to tell who's who. And-and these insurgents hide behind they own kids and stuff. They cowards, y'know.

ALMA: Looka here, Mister Powell, and Condi they know what they talking 'bout when they say we gotta fight over there, right? After all they two black folks, plus they Christians, right?

LOUISE: Slow down, slow down—

ALMA:—So where are these "weapons" of mass" ...whattheycallit—so WHERE are they? How we helping them people, if we doing what Moni says we doing?

LOUISE: She's not doing it.

ALMA: *(Pointing to pages in* LOUISE's *hands)* She say *right there* that she done run over a baby in the street!

*(*ALMA *and* LOUISE *stop and lock eyes.)*

ALMA: Now that's something I could see Whites do, but not "Us".

*(*LOUISE *starts to hand the papers back to* ALMA.*)*

ALMA: You ain't finished.

*(*LOUISE *reads on.)*

LOUISE: "Raped"?

ALMA: Two women going to use the "porta pot" at night.

LOUISE: Jesus.

ALMA: And who did it? The same guys they fight alongside of during the day!!!

(LOUISE *grabs* ALMA.)

LOUISE: Let's pray...

ALMA: Child, after I called you, I went straight back out to Greenfield Plaza. That Recruiter, Sergeant Wilson? He been "reassigned" down somewhere's down South. (*Pause*) Now. Read *this*.

LOUISE: Let's pray...

ALMA: *My* letter to the Army, to the Officers! They better put my daughter back behind the desk like they said she would be!

LOUISE: They might read this letter and what if you make it worse for her? *Think* now. Think. All we can do is pray for Monique. Listen to me, Alma. We just plain, ordinary folks. We don't run the world. Best we can do is leave it in the hands of The Lord.

(ALMA *steps into a spotlight.* LOUISE *exits.*)

ALMA: "Dear Sweetheart: make sure you carry a knife.. at all...times. Salute with a knife hidden on you, go to bed with that knife, walk that base with your knife..."

(ALMA *moves into another spotlight.*)

Scene

(MONIQUE *enters with her head covered in bandages, slowly groping her way, blindly.*)

MONIQUE: Momma???

(ALMA *rushes to* MONIQUE, *holding her, helping her to sit.*)

ALMA: Hey, Sweet! Thought you were napping....

MONIQUE: Where'd you go?

ALMA: How was your nap, sweetie? (*Holding her*)

MONIQUE: Dreamt I was smelling those lilies in the backyard. And then oranges. Woke up with the scent of oranges, then it faded into "facts."

(ALMA *rocks* MONIQUE.)

ALMA: (*Rocking*) Fact is, you my beloved girl, and I'm so grateful to have you back.

MONIQUE: I *did* things over there.

ALMA: We looking straight ahead and into the future, we not dwelling on what's past.

MONIQUE: What future? Guess you could say Jesus paid me back, huh.

ALMA: We not gonna have that kinda talk, now. Hear me?!

MONIQUE: Where you been?

ALMA: Got groceries so we stocked up. Went over the fill out more of them damn veterans papers...checked at the church office 'bout the Fund, we still getting in checks, how 'bout that!?

(ALMA *slaps* MONIQUE's *palm in celebration.*)

MONIQUE: You went to see him, did you?

ALMA: Wha?

MONIQUE: Terry. Didn't you?

ALMA: You asked me not to.

MONIQUE: When have you ever done what I asked.

ALMA: Girl, stop.

MONIQUE: *(Mocking)* "Girl, stop!" You did, didn't you?

ALMA: Monique.

MONIQUE: Swear you didn't go over there. Swear on your Bible.

ALMA: Let's put on *Oprah*...

MONIQUE: Couldn't help yourself but to go over there on his job, begging and pleading!!!!

(MONIQUE gropes her way over to ALMA, *clinging to her.)*

ALMA: Never mind, all that,now...

MONIQUE: Never—so, you *DID* DO IT!! You went groveling for him to "please" get back together with the "mutant" now that she's had her face blown to smithereens.

ALMA: You're still a lovely young woman.. And guess what? He asked about you so nice...he was glad to see me...and...and

(MONIQUE pushes ALMA *away.)*

MONIQUE: GET AWAY AND STAY AWAY!

(MONIQUE gropes her away from ALMA, *flaying her arms for* ALMA *to keep away.)*

ALMA: Please...please... Don't be like this,now... Talk to me! What was like over there? Talk to me like when you wrote me...Moni, please. Please, I'm so sorry. Looka here...from now on I quit meddling. You and Terry that's your business...this time I really, really promise...

MONIQUE: No man on earth gonna want to be with a "freak."

ALMA: We not having that kinda talk, Monique! Now you a strong woman and-and-and you gonna lead a good life, understand me!? Monique?

(Silence)

MONIQUE: Killers don't deserve mercy.

ALMA: Whatever you did, Jesus forgives you.

(MONIQUE *gropes her way offstage.*)

MONIQUE: Your Jesus forgives me.

(ALMA *watches* MONIQUE *go. Sound of slamming door. Silence)*

(Silence. ALMA *stares out as lights shift.)*

Scene

(Lights shift-gospel choir is heard—morning of the funeral.)

(LOUISE *and* VIOLA *emerge from the shadows in choir robes, singing. Grief-stricken)*

(Pause. ALMA *in a daze)*

ALMA: Her first week home was to be her last. Yes, yes, Reverend, you done tole me that God only "gives us what we can bear." *(Pause)* But see, Monique couldn't bear to live out the rest of her days on this earth thinking she was a stitched up "freak" turning people's heads. So don't blame her. *(Pause)* She's the one who had to live with it on the inside. What it feel like from the inside?!! Maybe if I had raised her like my Momma raised me—took a strap to her growing up, make her too scared to make up her own mind...maybe then she would've heeded me and not gone over there... No. No. *(Pause)* Truth is...seemed like a bargain. Her college. Me debt free. Ha. "Debt free." *(Pause)* Church, I can't cry on the outside. Inside, I'm a river overflowing, but outside.. all I can do is call on Je-sus!!

Je-sus!! *(Pause)* Yes, I know this the House of the Lord!
(Pointing) All Southwest Detroit admire my strength in
spite of my grief... But I must have no bitterness... See
it would be acceptable to everybody if I was to collapse
over the casket—I'm supposed to be bowing my
head, in supplication to the will of the Almighty. But
I'm—outraged, damn it! She wrote me, Church. Stench
of rotting bodies—broken babies buried in rubble—
faceless people wrapped in black robes and smattered
into teeny, tiny pieces just cause they all look the same
to "us".

(We hear uncomfortable coughing from "Congregation".)

*(LOUISE and VIOLA signal each other, LOUISE starts to
approach ALMA.)*

ALMA: Brother Dyson! Don't let your son go over there!
Stop him! Don't listen to what they promise you!!!
Brother and Sister Taylor, don't let your child go over
there!!! Tell them to go A-WOL with your blessings!

(Responding to a comment in audience)

ALMA: "Easy for me to say?!" NO, IT'S NOT EASY
FOR ME TO SAY, MY DAUGHTER'S FACE IS THE
DOWN PAYMENT!! *(Turning on* LOUISE*)* Stay right
where you are. I will NOT sit back down. *(Then to us)*
AND DON'T TELL ME 'BOUT NO "INSURGENTS",
DON'T TELL ME 'BOUT NO...GOD-LESS A-RABS...
'cause I know mothers now, Church. I feel those other
mothers, church. I'm—I'm—

*(LOUISE and VIOLA nod to unseen people and start to drag
ALMA offstage.)*

ALMA: Stay back! STAY BACK!! My daughter, my child
gave her face!! My child, was the first black woman in
America to give her whole face for democracy, people!!

(LOUISE *and* VIOLA *stand back, awkward, not knowing what to do next. Again, they attempt to take* ALMA *off the stage.*)

ALMA: —so don't be putting ya hands on me!!! (*Calling to unseen figure*) DON'T COME UP TO ME, REVEREND!! (*As if correcting him*) YES, THIS IS THE TIME AND PLACE, THE PROPER PLACE— Only the mothers with faceless children can touch me. Only mothers over there with faceless, blown up, shot up, beat up children, mothers with "insurgent" children, mothers bloody with they son's blood, with they daughters raped to death, other mothers over here with they children coming back broken, maimed, with they violated minds...ONLY MOTHERS OF WAR CORPSES EVERYWHERE CAN PUT THEY HANDS ON ME. Why couldn't I know what was coming? Why couldn't I know to help her escape, why couldn't I protect her, Louise?!

(*The gospel choir starts up with a full, rousing song, drowning* ALMA *out.*)

ALMA: LISTEN TO ME!!

Scene

(ALMA *stands in spotlight. The past—morning*)

(*Silence, then sound of a bus engine starting up*)

(MONIQUE *enters in jeans and jean jacket, carrying a duffel bag. They hug,* MONIQUE *turns to go,* ALMA *grabs her.*)

ALMA: Don't go.

MONIQUE: (*Smiling*) Momma, now, c'mon now. People are watching.

ALMA: To hell with that.

MONIQUE: *(Playful)* You cursing? *(Then serious)* C'mon, now, help me be brave. You promised you'd be brave. *(Pause, she kisses* ALMA.*)* I'll be back, and in school. Then Terry and me married.

*(*ALMA *hugs* MONIQUE *tighter.)*

ALMA: Oh, I love you so!! *(Pause)* I'll be praying everyday, all day, day in and day out.

(A special spotlight illuminates MONIQUE's *pretty face.* ALMA *caresses* MONIQUE's *face. Gospel music fades up, loud, then blackout.)*

MONIQUE: That's what you do, Momma. You keep your prayers coming. You pray.

(Sound of the gospel choir comes up strong. Fade out)

END OF PLAY

SON

CHARACTERS & SETTING

CRAIG, *African-American man, late 30s*
MONA, CRAIG's *wife, Italian-American, late 30s*
SYBIL, CRAIG's *mother, African-American, 65 or older*
GRACE, CRAIG's *sister, African-American 32*

Play takes place in two places: a "room" inside CRAIG's *head, and an upstairs farmhouse bedroom.*

Time: Late summer—2009

Scene

(Setting: Two basic areas. The upstage area is a Mental Space inside CRAIG'S *head. There sits a tanned colored, plush leather swivel chair with arm rests.)*

(The downstage area is the bedroom of a farmhouse with one simple rocking chair and perhaps a small chest to sit on.)

(At rise: The swivel chair in spotlight)

(A man seated in a tanned colored, plush leather swivel chair with his back to the audience. He wears a headset, and we hear murmured voices as if coming from his headset. A moment, then the man swivels around in the chair and faces us.)

(It is CRAIG, *dressed in formal white pants, and with an undershirt.)*

(A tiny beeping sound is heard as if coming off the swivel chair.)

CRAIG: *(Into his headset, softly)* Tracking target...tracking target! *(There is a moment as he watches an imaginary screen placed directly in front of his face.)* TARGET HIT!! Bullseye! *(Then in a moment)* Fuck! Fuck! "Payload" fuck up. Do you read? Over... *(He rises, rips off his headset, flings it into the swivel chair. Freezes)*

(Sound of an outdoor violin playing a lilting romanic melody. The echo of a woman's voice is heard. CRAIG *looks about as if through ether.)*

MONA: *(Calling from offstage)* Craig? Honey? Sweetheart?? *(She enters dressed in a lovely formal dress with a pink corsage, and high heels. She carries a tray with a mug of coffee and donuts. She studies him, smiling broadly.)* Well, hello....sleepy head...

CRAIG: *(Still dazed)* Uh-huh...

MONA: Darling, this is wonderful. Finally a prescription that worked.

(Groggy, blinking, CRAIG circles the leather swivel chair, MONA doesn't notice.)

CRAIG: Where are we?

(MONA places the tray of coffee and donuts onto the small chest downstage. She addresses CRAIG as if he is standing next to her.)

CRAIG: Where are we?

MONA: Maybe tonight we'll give you just half a pill, what'd you think? Since you've slept so well, now.

(CRAIG crosses back to MONA.)

CRAIG: We're at Momma's...in Ohio...Grace is getting—

MONA: *(Slightly disquieted)* Wow. "Sandman" really took you into "Dreamland", didn't he?

CRAIG: You've done all the driving...I've done all the sleeping.

MONA: No problem with that. Now you're totally rested. For once. Let's cross our fingers just half a dose might get you through the night.

CRAIG: Right.

MONA: Here. Coffee. Donuts...get something in your stomach.

(MONA pats CRAIG's cheek, he puts on his tux jacket.)

CRAIG: Everybody ready? Hey, where's Lizzie?

(MONA pins on CRAIG's corsage.)

MONA: All dressed, and chomping on her pacifier. Just have to keep her preoccupied until her cue.

(CRAIG *crosses to the front of the stage, looks out onto the audience as if out of a second story window.* MONA *joins him.*)

CRAIG: Dang, Momma got the whole town here, looks like.

MONA: Most of the town IS your family....

CRAIG: She was right to rent a big tent... Lookit Lizzie...

(CRAIG *calls out in the tone of speaking to a small child.* CRAIG *and* MONA *both wave.*)

CRAIG: (*Calling out*) Hey, Sweetpea! Aren't you pretty! You ready for Auntie Grace's wedding? Daddy loves you, baby! (*To* MONA) Look at her....

MONA: (*Looking*) Everybody wants to hold her...

CRAIG: Looks like she'll never know what it is to be shy.

MONA: She's a flirt...like her Dad.

CRAIG: (*Playful*) Me?! False accusation, I protest.

MONA: So. *This* is the "old homestead".

CRAIG: Yep.

MONA: Too bad we didn't get married here when we had our chance.

CRAIG: What chance? With me stationed in Heideberg?

(*Laughing,* MONA *impulsively kisses* CRAIG *hard on the mouth.*)

CRAIG: Mummmm. What'd I do to deserve that?

MONA: (*Laughing*) Don't you just LOVE, LOVE weddings! Everybody hopeful for the bride and groom...everybody gathered in goodwill to celebrate hope....

(CRAIG *suddenly grabs hold of the rocking chair, sits in it, and starts rocking back and forth.*)

(MONA *waves out the window, calls out.*)

MONA: *(Calling)* Hi, Auntie Myrtle! We're coming right down! *(Turns to* CRAIG*)* Ready, honey?

(MONA *sees that* CRAIG *is rocking back and forth, his eyes closed.*)

MONA: Baby, don't get too comfortable. The music has started,

CRAIG: Baby, you go on down, mix and mingle. I'll join you in a few...

MONA: Sweetheart...you're the "shining knight" that your relatives always want to see, I'm just "back up"...

(CRAIG *continues to rock in the rocker, his eyes shut.*)

CRAIG: Don't say that...whew... *now*, I feel better! Now, I can collect myself.

MONA: Honey, you're going to wear that chair out....

CRAIG: Collect myself. Keep the bad dreams off...

MONA: Not more bad dreams!

CRAIG: Look, all I need to concentrate on now, is to not fight with my goddamn father in public...

MONA: Don't let him bait you! Okay? When he starts in about his "tour of duty" in Vietnam, back away. Especially today. Promise?

(CRAIG *breathes deeply, and continues to rock back and forth in the chair.*)

CRAIG: Just give me ten minutes in this, and I'll be good to go... *(He calls into the air.)* Right, Ma Rose?

MONA: Excuse me?

CRAIG: *(Smiling)* Baby, it's okay...it's okay...don't weird-out...growing up, this old antique saved me.

Would always get me back on track. Especially after one of the old man's whippings, man. Never mind.

MONA: What?! Your father beat you?

(*As* CRAIG *continues to rock back and forth in the chair, eyes shut*)

CRAIG: Mona, help me out, okay? Just give me a few minutes "solo".

MONA: My, God, Craig I mean...I might get a slap on the wrist, maybe when I disobedied, but I never was..

CRAIG: Now, don't .go smearing your eye-shadow, it was never that bad. And he never touched me while my Ma Rose was alive.

MONA: Yeah, but your great-grannie died when you were seven. Some help.

CRAIG: To hell with "memory lane" —we're supposed to be celebrating.

MONA: You're the one wearing that rocker into ground, not me.

(SYBIL *and* GRACE *enter.* SYBIL *wearing a formal dress and corsage.* GRACE *wears a bridal gown without the veil.. Both are in a state of panic.* CRAIG *leaps up from the rocker.*)

CRAIG: Momma, whatsamatter? Baby Sis, you look gorgeous, girl! Lookit my Baby Sis as a Bride!

GRACE: (*Panic*) Daddy's not coming.

(CRAIG *stops cold.*)

CRAIG: Not coming? What you mean not coming?

(*Silence,* GRACE *and* SYBIL *too upset to speak*)

CRAIG: This is his daughter's wedding, of course he's coming.

MONA: Of course he's coming.

CRAIG: Momma, hold on...what'd you mean Dad's not coming?

(SYBIL *shoves her cellphone into* CRAIG's *face*)

SYBIL: Text message from that "Son-of-a -Blank-Blank!" *You* read it.

(CRAIG *reads the cellphone screen.*)

CRAIG: Bitch. Let me get that bastard on the phone...

SYBIL: What good will that do, he can't fly here in twenty minutes.

GRACE: *(To* CRAIG*)* And you'll only end up screaming at each other. Momma, take away all the flowers Daddy sent, throw 'em in the garbage.

SYBIL: Baby, we don't have time to separate the flowers—just try and concentrate on everybody else's bouquets.

GRACE: *(To* MONA*)* What I wanna do right now is...is... grab a great, great, big bowl of chips, and a cold beer on tap, and hide out..

MONA: But, you won't.

SYBIL: *(To* MONA, *slightly testy) Of course, she won't.*

CRAIG: Grace, you deserve a beautiful ceremony, and that's what you're gonna—

SYBIL: Amen! You're big brother here, is gonna make sure you have it.

GRACE: And Barry what will he say? His mother and daddy, his sister—we all *know* she—thinks Barry's making the wrong choice...

SYBIL: *(To* GRACE*)* Sh-h-h-h...she's just jealous cause you'll be the prettiest one in that whole family...

CRAIG: *(To* GRACE*)* Baby girl, take it from me, you gotta learn to dismiss these in-laws, man.

GRACE: And now my hair won't cooperate! and my shoes are too tight....

(SYBIL*l fidgets with the hem of* GRACE'*s dress.*)

SYBIL: Stand still...make sure we got this hem right...

GRACE: *(To* CRAIG *and* MONA*)* And Barry's not ever met Daddy, and now Daddy...!!!

CRAIG: Fuck that bastard.

SYBIL: Son, please, your language...no...nevermind, you go 'head, call it like it is...

CRAIG: Not even the decency to—do you believe it! Text Message, of all the—At the last minute! Mister "Macho-old school-Army" ...This cuts the knot, everybody!

(MONA *reads the cellphone screen.*)

MONA: Well, if his wife has tripped—and broken her ankle...

SYBIL: Mona, now you've been in this family long enough to know how that third wife has got him just—just—

CRAIG: Pussy-whipped. Excuse me, Momma.

SYBIL: Naw-naw, in this case, you go right ahead.

CRAIG: "Her ankle." Like they've never heard of "crutches"?

GRACE: I can't believe he's bailing out on me!

CRAIG: Now, when he raised us, and was living with you, Momma, he was all "iron fist". It don't make sense that he'd now let this new woman dictate—

SYBIL: Honey, he "married" himself—it makes perfect sense.

MONA: Meanwhile, everybody, we just move on to Plan B.

CRAIG: I'll be walking Grace down the aisle. Plan B.

MONA: Exactly. Craig is right here. That's what we focus on.

(A soft beeping sound seems to come from the leather swivel chair. CRAIG startles, he stares up at the swivel chair, he is the only one who hears the sound, or who sees the chair.)

(CRAIG gives his head a slight shake, the beeping stops.)

GRACE: What would I do without my Big Brother.

SYBIL: Craig's the real man in this family, always has been.

GRACE: But, Barry's parents—

MONA: We will say that your father's had an emergency, just like he says he has. Only we'll say that *he's* the one who had to go to the hospital—say—for his heart ...

SYBIL: What "heart"?

MONA: ...Or something... And we go forward.

GRACE: I wanna swallow down every one of these donuts—whole...

MONA: But you won't.

SYBIL: *(To MONA) Of course, she won't.*

CRAIG: *(To GRACE)* Hey, now, Big Bro will always take care of you...

(A soft beeping sound comes from the upstage swivel chair, CRAIG is drawn to the chair, as he tries to shake the sound shakes it off.)

GRACE: Plus, me and Barry had a squabble last night over something stupid.

MONA: Couples always do that, girl. That's so universal, it's like, a scrape before the wedding is good luck.

SYBIL: Hummp. In my day, couples didn't shack up together before going to the altar... never mind... never mind.

(Beeping continues then, begins to subside. CRAIG rejoins them downstage, ever cheerful.)

MONA: *(To GRACE, and CRAIG)* Your brother and I had a mighty good row the night before we got hitched, didn't we?

CRAIG: *(To MONA, playful)* Hell, the prospect of facing your Sicilian uncles, man...

GRACE: Worse thing is, I didn't get a wink of sleep all night. *(To everyone)* Does it show?

(MONA holds GRACE's face in her hands, to check her makeup.)

MONA: Lemme look. And let's see what can do to refix this hair...

SYBIL: *(To MONA)* Her hair is something for me to handle, honey.

MONA: I can help. And your makeup, let's see…

SYBIL: *(To MONA)* You attend to Craig, I'll get Grace repaired.

CRAIG: Let her help Momma, we don't have time for all this! The family, and most of this hick town is all gathered on the back field.

(GRACE and SYBIL attend to GRACE's hair, earrings, dress...)

GRACE: Such a blessing you guys got here right in time.

MONA: Such a blessing Craig's on vacation.

CRAIG: Mona's the one who put the "pedal to the metal", man.

SYBIL: But, why not fly? It's such a long trip.

CRAIG: No flights for me. Work with enough planes day in, and day out. Sick of planes. Anyways, <u>now</u>... now...I'm walking my sister down the aisle...the Bride...

(SYBIL *crosses to the "window" facing the audience. She makes broad gestures to someone. She flashes all ten fingers, as in "ten minutes more".*)

GRACE: I so promised Barry we'd be on time.

MONA: *(To* GRACE*)* Barry's gonna take one look at you, and time will stand still.

GRACE: *(Quietly to* MONA*)* Just as long as he doesn't start in on the cocktails...

(CRAIG *takes* GRACE *to one side.*)

CRAIG: Hey. It's none of my business... But... You sure you wanna "jump" this "broom"?

SYBIL: *(Stepping right in)* Of course, she's sure.

GRACE: *(A bit more tenuous)* Of course, I'm sure.

SYBIL: Barry's got a great promotion, and Grace, here, going on for her degree. Of course, she's sure, right Grace? *(She sees a signal from someone out the window.)* All clear, Everybody. Grace, I want you to let yourself relax.

(CRAIG *stops, stunned, his smile drops, no one else notices this.*)

CRAIG: *(To himself)* All clear... "All clear on the ground..." All clear...

(CRAIG *crosses upstage and re-circles the swivel chair, no one notices.*)

SYBIL: *(To* MONA*)* Mona, d'you make sure Lizzie's wearing her training panties?

MONA: I *do* remember that my daughter's only two years old, Sybil. *(Brightly)* Okay, Everybody, here comes the "Bride!"

(CRAIG *continues to circle the unseen swivel chair.*)

CRAIG: Here comes, the...bride..! Here comes, the...
bride..!

GRACE: *(To* SYBIL*)* Am I flushed? Do I look flushed?

SYBIL: *(To* GRACE*)* C'mon...get your veil....

(SYBIL *and* GRACE *start to exit off,* SYBIL *stops.*)

SYBIL: Nunno! Wait! Everybody, hold hands. C'mon...!

(*They all join hands, shut their eyes, and bow their heads.*
CRAIG *reopens his eyes, staring out.*)

SYBIL: *(Calling out)* Jesus, we ask your blessings on
this family, on this day. *(She suddenly pauses, notices
something on the floor, bends over, picks it up.)* That
Cleaning Woman... I don't call this vacumming... *(She
closes her eyes, resumes.)* Jesus, we ask your blessings on
us this day... And, Ma Rose? We've all gathered back at
the old homestead before we sell it, Ma Rose, I couldn't
help it.. Taxes are too high.. Grace'll be the last family
member to be married at the "Old Place."

SYBIL: *(Still praying)* The family's all well, and healthy,
Ma Rose. Craig is doing well, married, living in
Nevada, has the cutest little dollbaby girl you'd ever
want to see—

CRAIG: *(Whispering)* Momma, c'mon, we gotta hurry
up.

SYBIL: *(Still praying)* ...'Course mixed race babies are
looked upon differently then we you raised me...

(MONA *startles, opens her eyes, locks eyes with* CRAIG, *who
sighs.*)

MONA: What?!

(*Violin music starts up,* GRACE *gestures towards the
window.*)

GRACE: Mom, I'm late enough as it is!

SYBIL: *(Rushing)* Bless us with your spirit in Jesus'
name, Amen

CRAIG: *(Jovial)* Okay, People! Showtime...!

(SYBIL and GRACE rush off.)

MONA: *(To CRAIG)* What was that about "mixed race..."

(CRAIG hurriedly kisses MONA.)

CRAIG: Sweetheart, I gotta concentrate...shit, I came to
just be a witness—now I've gotta walk her down the—
fucking...fuck...

MONA: Something wrong?

*(CRAIG straigthen's his tie in the mirror, MONA smooths
her dress.)*

CRAIG: All I have to do is walk her down the aisle. Take
her arm. Walk her down the aisle, hand her to Barry.
That's all I have to do.

MONA: Something the matter?

CRAIG: *(Cheerful, determined)* Girl, I'm great, just great...
(Pauses, then) Oh, and uh... Sweetheart, listen...listen
up...

MONA: Umm- Mmmm... Let me guess,"If any one asks,
your work at the base is *top secret* and you don't wanna
talk about it."

(Off CRAIG's look)

MONA: You've only told me a billion times since we
left home, Darling.

(As CRAIG and MONA kiss.)

MONA: Is it really secret?

CRAIG: What's that?

MONA: Whatever you do at the base. Or is it that you
just don't want to "talk" about it? Whatever "it" is.

(CRAIG *rummages through a small tote bag propped on the floor chest. He pulls out a bottle of pills.*)

MONA: Craig...????!

CRAIG: Just one. Just one—so that I stay up on my feet.

(MONA *grabs the pill bottle before he can pull away, she studies it, surprised, shocked.*)

CRAIG: Just one. This way I can gear myself up.

MONA: You're not supposed to combine these with sleeping pills.

CRAIG: You worry too much, I gotta be at my best when I get down there.

(MONA *works to remain calm.*)

MONA: Where'd you get these Uppers, Sweetheart?

CRAIG: Look, I gotta pull this whole thing off!! *(Pause)* Okay, on the base, if you must know, okay?

MONA: On the base?!

(CRAIG *rushes over to the window, points.*)

CRAIG: *(Then)* Stop grilling me! I gotta get down there, and give my sister away! Already been to *one* wedding, and now I gotta come through for the family...!

MONA: What?

CRAIG: Huh?

MONA: What wedding?

CRAIG: What're you saying?

MONA: What'd you mean you've already been to "one wedding?"

CRAIG: What? What're you talking about?

MONA: I...I...never mind...I dunno...nothing. Now, I'm hearing things..

(CRAIG *takes* MONA*'s hand, they dash into a new spotlight that suggests bright sunshine.*)

(CRAIG *and* MONA, *stand arm in arm. Sounds of murmuring crowd.* CRAIG *and* MONA *wave and smile at unseen people.*)

(*Romantic violin music.* CRAIG *is visibly straining to calm himself.* MONA *pecks him on the cheek again, then moves to the side.*)

(*Enter* GRACE *in full veil, carrying a bridal bouquet.*)

(*Sound of audience applause.* GRACE *takes* CRAIG*'s arm.* SYBIL *moves in and takes a flash photo.*)

(*Flashbulbs go off,* MONA *steps in front of them, smiling, and takes a flash photo.* CRAIG *startles at each flash, straining to maintain his smile.*)

(*Suddenly:* CRAIG *hears a slow, methodical beeping sound coming from the upstage swivel chair. Craig turns to face it. He turns back just as under the violin music.*)

CRAIG: (*Dazed*) ...target hit...target hit... NOW.

(*Violin music continues as,* CRAIG *turns and* GRACE *suddenly takes her bridal veil and holds it under her nose, covering her mouth, so that only her eyes are visible—as if wearing a traditional Muslim burka.*)

(CRAIG *screams a silent scream, freezes. beeping loud for a few beats. Lights out*)

(*Lights up*)

Scene

(The upstairs room—half-hour later)

(CRAIG, his tie unloosened, paces around the swivel chair... runs to the rocker. Sits, and starts rocking fiercely)

CRAIG: *(Calling to the air)* Ma Rose, help me. Help me. Help me...

(MONA enters.)

MONA: There you are... what're you doing inside? Everybody's looking for you.

CRAIG: What happened, what'd I do?

MONA: *(Very casual and happy)* Do? About what?

CRAIG: Did I—Mona, listen, just say, yes or no, okay?

MONA: Whats the matter, Sweetheart.

CRAIG: Just answer yes, or no.

MONA: About what?

CRAIG: Did I disgrace the family? I finked out, didn't I?

MONA: Craig, what'd you mean?

CRAIG: Did I give the bride away?

MONA: You mean, Grace?

CRAIG: WHO ELSE WOULD I MEAN?! What other bride is there!?

MONA: What is wrong?!

CRAIG: DID I get through the ceremony?! Correctly??

MONA: Of course you got through the ceremony, why wouldn't you?

CRAIG: *(Quietly bewildered)* Right.

MONA: Wasn't our Lizzie, darling? Tottling up with that ring pillow? I've got great shots... *(Her smile disappears.)* Constant sleeping pills, that don't work, and now, you're on speed.

CRAIG: Will you relax? All we gotta do is just keep it together...

MONA: Promise me you won't drink any drinks, on top of this, please.

(SYBIL enters, MONA and CRAIG break apart, putting on their "happy faces". SYBIL carries a camcorder.)

SYBIL: Well, y'all, Grace has finally been made an honest woman—

MONA: *(Very bright)* Grace was a bride out of a dream. Wasn't Lizzie marvelous?

SYBIL: The cutest thing you'd ever wanna see—told you two years old wasn't too young... *(She addresses the air.)* Oh, Ma Rose, if you could've seen your sweet great-great Grandbaby today!! *(She collapses onto the rocker, removing her heels.)* Aw, lemme rest my poor bunions.

(SYBIL detects tension.)

SYBIL: Oh, 'cuse me, am I interrupting something?

CRAIG: *(Buoyant)* Just your Son practicing my speech to toast our Bride.

(SYBIL goes to the window in her stocking feet.)

SYBIL: *(Calling out)* Hey, Ruby!!! START CALLING FOLKS TO SIT DOWN TO THE TABLES..

(SYBIL turns back to CRAIG, MONA monitors CRAIG anxiously.)

SYBIL: *(To CRAIG)* Uncle Leroy say word's going round that you're doing top secret "terrorist protection services" —out there in Nevada.

CRAIG: *(Swiftly)* Don't wanna talk about it.

SYBIL: Well naturally, if it's top secret.

CRAIG: *(To* MONA*)* Didn't you tell people that I didn't want to talk about it?

MONA: *(Pointed)* Darling, *you* were the one boasting about it, *not me.*

SYBIL: Son you look so hot, and tense...you alright?

MONA: He hasn't been sleeping very well these last few months.

CRAIG: *(Rallying)* Hey, that's all over and done with. We're on vacation, I'm on R and R...c'mon, y'all, let's toast my Baby Sister!

*(*SYBIL *glances out the window.)*

SYBIL: What a great shot of the tent, and everybody from this angle... *(She takes camcorder and begins recording out the window.)*

(As soon as SYBIL *does so a beeping sound comes from the upstage swivel chair.)*

SYBIL: I'm gonna be a movie director yet, y'all...

CRAIG: Turn that thing off!!!

*(*SYBIL *inadvertantly turns the camcorder on* CRAIG, *he steps away.)*

CRAIG: Get that thing away from me!!

(Beeping stops. SYBIL *and* MONA *exchange baffled looks, just as...)*

*(*GRACE, *enters in bridal dress, no veil.)*

GRACE: *(To* CRAIG*)* Hey, you! Am I gonna get toasted? We're all about to sit down to eat. *(She kisses* CRAIG.*)* Thanks for saving the day, Big Bro. And you get an extra A-plus for being such a big hit with Lorraine.

CRAIG: Who's Lorraine?

GRACE: My new mother-in-law, silly. You were so charming with her.

CRAIG: Was I?

SYBIL: She's the big-breasted woman with the loud lipstick—

GRACE: *(To* SYBIL*)* Mother! She's my new family! *(Then)* Mona, thanks for helping to make Barry's Boss feel right at home...

*(*MONA *is so anxiously focused on* CRAIG, *she barely realizes what she is saying.)*

MONA: No problem, just send all the white people to me.

(The others all "look" at MONA. *She suddenly takes this in.)*

MONA: What? What is it?

SYBIL: Let's go eat and mingle, Everybody...

MONA: Wait. Everybody...let's kiss the beautiful beautiful bride! *(To* GRACE*)* You were *so* lovely out there.

(Beeping sound heard only by CRAIG, *resumes as* SYBIL *and* MONA *applaud* GRACE, *who beams.)*

GRACE: *(To* MONA*)* Did you notice? No snacking out of me, sticking with my diet.

CRAIG: *(Suddenly in response to beeping)* GET HER OFF TARGET!!

(The women stop cold, staring at him. MONA *leaps into action.)*

MONA: *(To* GRACE *and* SYBIL*)* He's over heated. He's got to get out of the "target" of the heat. *(To* CRAIG*)* Right, honey? *(To* GRACE *and* SYBIL*)* You guys go on, Grace, everybody will be looking for the Bride. He just needs to splash some water on this face.

SYBIL: *(To* MONA*)* Well, y'all hurry. *(Suddenly)* Oh, my God... *(To* GRACE*)* did we sit Cousin Louise next to Charlotte?

(SYBIL *and* MONA *hurry out.*)

CRAIG: Tracking target! Tracking... (*He covers his mouth. He starts pacing.*)

MONA: What in the world...?! And now, we're back to what happens when you get home at night...

CRAIG: I'm okay. I'm back...

MONA: "Back"? From where? Are you going to get help? How long do I have to beg and plead, Craig?

(SYBIL *enters, rushed.*)

SYBIL: Son? Everybody's waiting... Oh, and you'll never guess—Stanley and Louise are back together again, after putting us all through that messy divorce, can you believe it!?

(CRAIG *pulls out his cell phone, shows* SYBIL.)

CRAIG: Momma, I—I—I—just got a call from back in Nevada...yeah, back on the base...

MONA: (*To* CRAIG) You *what*? *When*?

SYBIL: Nothing bad, I hope?

CRAIG: Got an emergency on my hands. Uh-uh-uh... Gotta call them back. Sorry, Uncle Leroy'll have to do the honors.

SYBIL: Awww. Terrorist stuff, huh? (*She turns to* MONA.)

MONA: (*Playing along to* SYBIL) Oh, yes. I'll stay right here in case he needs me. Are the caterers serving up everything like you asked? Go make sure.

(SYBIL *starts to run off.*)

CRAIG: Bride off target...bride off target... (*He instantly covers his mouth, shocked.*)

SYBIL: (*To* MONA) What's he mumbling?

MONA: Sybil, he's so overtired, and overworked from his job...and—uh...he's...he's got this call coming in... but—but you've got everything else to deal with... never mind Craig, I'm here for him...

(CRAIG *continues to circle the swivel chair.*)

(SYBIL *goes to the window*)

SYBIL: *(Calling out the window)* Grace!! Honey, your brother's got some emergency call from Nevada, Sweetheart. Uh-huh. Have Uncle Leroy do the toast. Humm-hum...Craig's so sorry about this... *(Pause)* ...oh, no, Leroy's too tipsy?!

(SYBIL *turns back to* CRAIG—*beeping starts, only* CRAIG *can hear it...*)

SYBIL: Leroy's already too tipsy. Oh, my goodness....

(CRAIG *stumbles forward.*)

CRAIG: Nevermind, a killer can give a toast, that's perfectly normal...

(CRAIG *is horrified by what has come out of his mouth.* SYBIL *stops him bewildered, she exchanges a confused look with* MONA, *who is bewildered and embarassed.*)

MONA: *(To* SYBIL*)* Sybil, don't let Uncle Leroy start up! Grace is depending on us.

(SYBIL *hurries to the window.*)

SYBIL: *(Calling out)* Myrtle!! Have Reggie take Leroy into the barn till he... Yeah! That's right! Tell Ruby to have Reuben do the toast... Good...

(CRAIG *leaps into the rocker,* SYBIL *turns, and watches as he fiercely rocks back and forth.*)

SYBIL: *(Back to* MONA*)* Mona, what's wrong?

MONA: Fatigue. The heat. He's going to take a nap.

SYBIL: But, he's on call, for that emergency call...

MONA: (*Frazzled*) You keep saying Craig is for <u>me</u> to take care of! So, leave us. Please.

(CRAIG *rocks fiercely.*)

CRAIG: Ma Rose, help me. Help me. HELP ME.

MONA: Craig, honey, sweetheart...sh-h-h-h, you're just coming down..

SYBIL: "Coming down" from what? Mona, what in the world....????

(CRAIG *crosses to the swivel chair, struggles not to put on the headphones in the chair. The women relate to him as if he still sits in the rocker.*)

CRAIG: (*Dazed*) Ma Rose, don't make me go back! Don't make me go back!

SYBIL: (*To* MONA) This don't sound like "fatigue" to me.

MONA: Can't you just leave us be? You've got a whole wedding to—

SYBIL: Excuse me??? This is my SON!!!

(CRAIG, *as if controlled by an invisible force, places the headphones on.*)

CRAIG: I'm at THIS wedding...not THAT wedding... THIS wedding...! No...NO...I'm at THAT wedding.... THAT's the wedding...THAT'S THE WEDDING I'M AT!!!!

(SYBIL *mimes shaking* CRAIG's *shoulders as if he is sitting in the rocker.*)

SYBIL: Oh, God. Sweet Jesus, he's on drugs!!!

MONA: He only took one, so it's not so bad.

SYBIL: One of what? Don't you tell me Craig Stanley Harris is on cocaine?!

MONA: Don't be ridiculous

SYBIL: Girl, who you calling "ridiculous"!!??

(CRAIG *freezes, staring out.*)

CRAIG: Ma Rose?! Ma Rose?!

(CRAIG *is as if catatonic, locked inside a shell.*)

MONA: We have to calm down. That's the first thing—if we panic, it's not going to help—

SYBIL: Don't you tell me to calm down, *you* calm down!

(CRAIG *leaps up from the swivel chair, still wearing the headphones, beeping continues, he speaks into the air.*)

CRAIG: I am NOT a killer!

SYBIL: Oh, God. Drug talk. He's hallucinating!

MONA: Calm down and let it run it's course.

SYBIL: Call an ambulance.

MONA: D'you want the rest of the family to know?

SYBIL: *You* got him hooked on—

MONA: Why don't you let him be just a "plain man" instead of a "golden God" for once!

CRAIG: I DON'T kill babies, and kids, and their Momma's and Daddies, and old folks—I DON'T massacre people at weddings! I DON'T!

(MONA *freezes.*)

MONA: What is he talking?

SYBIL: There has NEVER been no drug-mess in this family—at least not on my side.

(MONA *speaks into the rocking chair as if* CRAIG *has remained sitting there.*)

MONA: *(To* CRAIG*)* Craig, what do you have to tell me?

CRAIG: I don't kill babies.

SYBIL: Drug foolishness. *(To* MONA*)* And for you to know this is going on, and not tell me!

MONA: Let him talk!

(SYBIL *whirls on* MONA.)

SYBIL: I *know* you're not telling me what to do!

MONA: YOU try living with a damn sleepless machine who wakes up screaming in the middle of the night!

SYBIL: Craig always slept through the night when he was growing up.

CRAIG: (*Into the air*) Ma Rose, I didn't want to do it...no, I follow orders...I..I..

MONA: YOU watch him turn away from holding his own child! YOU watch him turn away his food, or if he eats, puke it right back up...

SYBIL: (*Shocked*) You mean, his taking drugs for something he's got?? Is it—it's not—terminal, or something? Oh, Jesus, you mean—he...he's—

(MONA *grabs hold of* SYBIL, *who is too frightened to speak. They watch* CRAIG.)

(CRAIG's *headphones begin beep softly, he stares straight out as if into a screen. Red lights shine on his face, as if coming off of a console.*)

CRAIG: (*To the air*) Ma Rose, you know I shouldn't've walked her down the aisle... That other bride's blood is ...thick on my hands....

MONA: (*To* CRAIG, *softly*) What other bride?

SYBIL: (*Paniced*) Stop hiding things from me, you two!! (*To* MONA) Is this a reaction to the medication they got him on?? How long has it got to live? Let me know the truth!

(CRAIG *circles* MONA *and* SYBIL *as if in a daze, smiling.*)

CRAIG: (*Into the air*) Only me and you...know, Ma Rose... See my air-conditioned bunker under ground?

(CRAIG *reaches his hand out and grasps an imaginary joystick. The red lights shine on his face.*)

SYBIL: His medication is driving him "koo-koo".

MONA: *(Realizing)* It's his...job!

CRAIG: ...Me on the hunt, Ma Rose ...sh-h-h-h-h-h... twenty-five thousand feet above their heads...you see it, don't you, Nana? ...Ready to launch my dove-white "bird" ...signal to satellite—joystick rotates in my hands...

SYBIL: *(To* MONA*)* How long did they give him— months? A year or two...?

(MONA *focuses entirely on* CRAIG, *realizing the truth.*)

CRAIG: Ma Rose, you just have to get used to the "feel" —be able to anticipate the two second delay...then you get good and it's seamless, YOU CAN OPERATE THE CAMERA SO EFFECTIVELY with practice

SYBIL: Mona!!!

MONA: Be quiet and get out.

SYBIL: This farmhouse has passed down through my family from slavery, and I *know* I'm not having no blond-blue-eyed...

CRAIG: ...MA ROSE!! Eight hours, ten hours, I send the PAYLOAD to delivery! I hunt down "roaches" ... I get to squash 'em from seventy-five hundred miles away, man! I get to snuff out any damn life I want! Me and my crew get to be GOD! *(He high fives into space.)*

MONA: *(To* SYBIL*)* So this is...is what he *really* does all day long.

SYBIL: Noncense, it's whatever meds you'll got him on...you can't launch something from twenty miles from Vegas to go half-way 'round the world.

(CRAIG *"pushes buttons" in air as he stares out.*)

CRAIG: Boom! *(He high fives some invisible crew member)* Way to go, man! Ha! I got the training, I'm ripped, man... They're all terrorists, shit. ALL HIGH VALUE TARGETS! They're all mutherfucking towel heads... Don't they suicide bomb, and shit? Don't they roadside bomb us!? Kill 'em all!! —so what if they got brides... and...guests...and kids...and babies...and cousins, and aunties, and uncles, and-and-fuck—YOU'RE ALL TERRORISTS CAUSE I SAY YOU ARE!! Even if you're a bride, you're probably a terrorist! YOU SHOULDN'T BE ON NO PROCESSION DOWN NO MOUNTAIN PASS! You'll never see who hit 'ya, ha!

(SYBIL attempts to shake CRAIG by the shoulders.)

SYBIL: *(To CRAIG)* Baby, it's Momma—come on back to me...

CRAIG: *(Into the air)* Ma Rose, first, they all look like spots on the ground—BOOM—then the camera comes in close—but the button is pushed, man, camera's in close up...it's wedding party—oh, shit...oh, well...splat goes the bride!! Splat goes the groom... Boom!

SYBIL: CRAIG! STOP MAKING THINGS UP. CRAIG!!! CRAIG!!!

(CRAIG whirls out of the dazed state, looks around. SYBIL and MONA stare at him, agape.)

CRAIG: Did we toast?

SYBIL: Are you terminally...ill. Sick? Tell me the truth!

(SYBIL runs to the window calls out. MONA locks eyes with CRAIG.)

SYBIL: BE RIGHT DOWN, Y'ALL...Craig's taking a nap. *(She turns to them.)* Tell me the truth.

CRAIG: *(To MONA)* What is she talking about?

MONA: *(To CRAIG)* So...you control remote control planes. That's what you really do?

CRAIG: *(Attempting to be recover)* Naw. Naw.

SYBIL: Never mind the planes. Are you healthy?

CRAIG: Momma, I'm in perfect condition. Just had a physical.

SYBIL: *(Bewildered)* But...Mona...said...

MONA: *(To CRAIG)* How many people died.

SYBIL: You can't push no button in Nevada, and—and—it's not possible.

MONA: HOW MANY PEOPLE.

(SYBIL whirls on MONA.)

SYBIL: YOU SHUT UP.

CRAIG: *(Dazed)* Ninety. Ninety people. Bride and groom, guests, and all their family...seventy-five hundred miles away. Last Friday. My shift. Bride did survive—what's left of her... Cameras let me see it all... up close and personal... Ninety people at a wedding, boom...

SYBIL: Nonsense. It don't make sense, it just don't make sense.

(CRAIG begins to cry.)

CRAIG: That's right, Momma. Don't believe it. You stay with normal, everyday America. With ya Walmarts, and ya Coscos and ya *Good Morning America*, and ya S U Vs and i-Pods, and fresh water from out of the tap, and cold beers out the keg...ALL of you.. Just floating in your bubbles.

MONA: *(To CRAIG)* Obviously, it was collateral damage. A mistake. You thought you detected terrorists ... you made a simple...

CRAIG: *(Mocking)* "Simple"!

MONA: ...A sad...mistake..!

CRAIG: How many "sad mistakes" can I live with every mutherfucking day? Mistakes in blasted flesh, and blood and bone all day long, then you expect to get home and help you shop for steak, and take Lizzie to the playground, and make love to you, and have a sound sleep...

SYBIL: Son, of course you naturally feel sorry for what you did. You're a sensitive soul. Just doing your duty. After all, those people are God-less. Well, I mean... that's not "what I mean", —you know I mean...

CRAIG: You're right! They don't bow to Jesus, they deserve what they get.

SYBIL: Now you stop! I DID NOT say that.

CRAIG: Do they deserve to have their babies blown up?

SYBIL: Then tell them to stop attacking us!! Those people did attack us on 9-11. So now, you let your heart rest easy.

CRAIG: THAT'S RIGHT, they're all towelheads. ALL NIGGAS LOOK ALIKE.

SYBIL: Don't you put words in my mouth! As mother I just—I just—

MONA: Craig, these people kill their own women, they blow up their own children...it's all over the news, everyday. They even send their own children out wearing bombs!

CRAIG: Right! They do things I don't understand, so it's good to blast 'em to kingdom come..

MONA: They come on our airplanes with bombs to kill us!

SYBIL: Right! Right! What are we supposed to be, "defenseless"? I'm surprised at you talking like this as a military man.

(CRAIG *salutes* MONA.)

CRAIG: I follow my orders. I do what I'm told. Flying over their terrority everyday, man, blasting whosoever I'm told to "blast". I am *loyal* to my country! ZOOM IN CAMERA. I'm a guardian angel.

MONA: These hardline terrorists want to take over the entire world—we must fight them. You know that's true.

(CRAIG *grabs* MONA *and pulls her to the window, gesturing out.*)

CRAIG: If a payload dropped outta the sky blasting any one of our families' babies, you'd see how quick any one of us turned"hardline terrorist".

(*Sound of applause coming from the window.* SYBIL *rushes over.*)

SYBIL: They're cutting the cake...

MONA: (*To* SYBIL) You should be with Grace.

(SYBIL *turns to* CRAIG.)

SYBIL: War is war. Period. These things happen in war..

CRAIG: Excuse me, Momma, but how the fuck do you know what "happens in war"? You wanna know WAR?! (*He grabs* SYBIL *and gestures into the air in front of them.*) Look into that console and you'll see what happens in war...

(SYBIL *and* MONA *only see empty space. They look at him confused.*)

SYBIL: Craig, please, please get a hold of yourself for my sake.

MONA: (*To* CRAIG) Sweetheart, we'll put in a request for you to get some help.

CRAIG: (*Re the empty space*) You can't see that??? Here...I got it here... Look! Look! (*He takes out, and holds out his i-Phone, operates the screen.*)

MONA: What is that doing on your cellphone??

CRAIG: *(To them both)* You wanna see war? You *sure* you wanna see *real* war?

(SYBIL grabs the phone.)

SYBIL: Please remember that you are a guest at your sister's wedding.

(SYBIL is about the hand the phone back to CRAIG, but glances down and gags.)

(MONA reaches for screen, SYBIL blocks her view.)

CRAIG: Okay, Momma—help me get *that* wedding out of my head, so I can be at my sister's wedding. Can ya do that? *(Refering to the screen)* See this Momma here?... Now, that's bits and chunks of her little girl or boy, that she's holding in her arms—

(SYBIL collapses, horrified.)

MONA: *(To CRAIG)* Don't do this to her.

CRAIG: Don't blame me! "It's the price of war..."

SYBIL: You show *them* pictures of *us*!! What *we* suffer at *their* hands!

CRAIG: Right! "What we suffer at *their* hands" is gonna help me go on downstairs, and fill up on the lobster dinner.

MONA: But sometimes you *do* kill the bad ones! Sometimes we do get it right!

(Suddenly, music from outside. They all pause.)

SYBIL: They'll be starting the dancing...

CRAIG: I say we kill every Arab woman we can get a hold of, that way there'll be no more "homegrown" terrorists, period.

(SYBIL slaps CRAIG across the mouth..)

SYBIL: You don't talk that way about people like that, I taught you better.

(MONA *attempts to grab the cellphone.* SYBIL *backs away with the phone.*)

SYBIL: *(To* MONA*)* Please don't. You have to live with your own child. Don't look.

CRAIG: When will I be able to hold my little girl in my lap, like I used to?

(SYBIL *tries to hold* CRAIG, *he pulls away, crying.*)

(*Suddenly we hear a recording of* The Jackson Five *singing,* I'll be There.)

MONA: *(To* CRAIG*)* Transfer!! Get out of this. Apply for a transfer!!

(GRACE *enters, still in bridal gown, no veil. She carries a tray with covered plates of food.*)

(*The music builds.*)

GRACE: What transfer? *(To* CRAIG*)* Still waiting for your call? We're dancing, everybody! You must be starving...

SYBIL: *(To* GRACE*)* Baby, the Bride is not supposed to serve folks at her own wedding. Listen uh...your brother's...uh...still busy with his..."emergency"...right Craig?

CRAIG: *(Buoyantly smiling to* GRACE*)* Can't come down yet, baby girl. I just can't.

MONA: *(To* GRACE, *re tray)* Girlfriend, you go on and, "part-tee" —we'll be down.

(GRACE *places the tray down. She suddenly grabs* CRAIG, *smiling, laughing, happy. She starts slow dancing with him to the sound of the music.*)

GRACE: Well, I'm gonna have my "big brother dance" right here, right now. "Terrorist protection", or not.

(Beeping starts to increase in CRAIG's *head as he dances with* GRACE, *the others hear nothing.)*

MONA: *(To* GRACE*)* How's my Lizzie holding up?

(Sound of MONA's *voice echoes inside* CRAIG's *head)*

MONA: *(V O, only heard by* CRAIG*)* How's my Lizzie holding up?

GRACE: She's playing with Tina's two-year-old. That Lizzie's such a charmer! And I checked, she's still "dry".

MONA: *(Actor and V O echoing)* Ha, oh, you're "practicing" for when it's *your* turn to be a "Mom"!

(Beeping sound loud...as a white light shines in on GRACE's *face, moving back and forth—the shape of a "cross" moves across her body as if she were a target in a telescopic lens.)*

*(*CRAIG *suddenly tackles* GRACE *to the ground.)*

CRAIG: SAVE THE BRIDE! ...SAVE THE BRIDE!..!! SAVE THE BRIDE!..!!

*(*GRACE *screams in shock.* SYBIL *leaps on* CRAIG *slapping at him to pull him off* GRACE. MONA *grabs for* SYBIL.*)*

CRAIG: GET DOWN, EVERYBODY!!! GET DOWN!!!

SYBIL: GET OFF HER! DON'T YOU TOUCH HER! IF YOU DON'T STOP THEY'LL LOCK YOU AWAY!! GET AWAY!

MONA: LEAVE HIM ALONE... DON'T HURT HIM—HE DOESN'T KNOW WHERE HE'S AT!!! HE DOESN'T KNOW!

(Silence. CRAIG *suddenly realizes what he is doing, he pulls* GRACE *up, hugs her tight.* SYBIL *backs away, shocked,* MONA *stands in agony.)*

GRACE: *(To* CRAIG, *terrified)* What is wrong with you?! *(To Mona and* SYBIL*)* What's wrong with Craig?

*(*MONA *gently caresses* CRAIG's *face.)*

CRAIG: Ma Rose help me cleanse my soul! Help me cleanse my soul....!

GRACE: Ma Rose?? *(To* MONA*)* What is wrong with my brother?

SYBIL: My son...my son...what they do to my boy...?

GRACE: "They" who? What is going on?!

(They all freeze in place, lights shift.)

*(*CRAIG *rises, grabs headphones from swivel chair, places them around his neck. Upbeat driven rhythmic military music. He beams, facing us, salutes.)*

CRAIG: *(To us)* Welcome to the elite ranks of our Unmanned Vehicle Training Program. My name is Major Craig Harris, and I'll be your instructor in unmanned reconnaissance. You'll be learning how we are able to remove enemy leadership, and militant targets with precise targeted technology...welcome aboard!

(The lights fade.)

END OF PLAY

www.ingramcontent.com/pod-product-compliance
Lightning Source LLC
Chambersburg PA
CBHW070026110426
42741CB00034B/2645